Dear Lillian

GENE EDWARDS

TYNDALE HOUSE PUBLISHERS, INC.
WHEATON, ILLINOIS

OTHER BOOKS BY GENE EDWARDS

Revolution: The Story of the Early Church
A Tale of Three Kings
The Inward Journey
The Divine Romance
Letters to a Devastated Christian
Our Mission
Preventing a Church Split
The Highest Life
Dear Lillian
The Prisoner in the Third Cell
The Secret to the Christian Life
The Chronicles of the Door
　　The Beginning
　　The Birth

Cover photo (Japanese Maples) copyright © 1981 by Lawrence S. Burr. Cover photo (pen) copyright © 1992 by Bill Bilsley. Parker Duofold Marbled Blue International Fountain Pen/Courtesy Parker Pen U.S.A. Ltd.

Unless otherwise indicated, Scripture quotations are taken from the *Holy Bible, New International Version.* Copyright © 1973, 1978, 1984 by International Bible Society. Used by permission of Zondervan Publishing House.

Library of Congress Cataloging-in-Publication Data
Edwards, Gene, date
　Dear Lillian / Gene Edwards
　　p.　　cm.
　Originally published: SeedSowers, © 1991.
　ISBN 0-8423-1078-9
　1. Death—Religious aspects—Christianity.　2. Future Life—
Christianity.　I. Title.
[BT825.E34　1992]　　　　　　　　　　　　92-15721
236'.1—dc20

Printed in the United States of America

99　98　97　96　95　94　93　92
　8　　7　　6　　5　　4　　3　　2　　1

🌿 *Lillian* is my wife's mother. She is ninety years old, and she is making plans to meet her Lord. One of the things that concerns her is the questions her grandchildren might have at the time of her death. She decided, therefore, that she would have a talk with each of them! In preparing to do this, she asked Helen and me to give her any insight we might have on the death of Christians and on things about the hereafter. Lillian has been a close friend of mine for about forty years now. Until my mother died, they, too, were good friends. The following letter is my contribution to Lillian's inquiry. I trust it will also be edifying to you.

Dear Lillian,

So you are planning to die soon, and you have some questions about what to say to your grandchildren about your death. Well, let's talk about it. But let's not begin with the question, *What will happen to Lillian after she is dead?* That is really the wrong place to begin. Instead, let's ask this question: *Where did Lillian begin?*

When did you, Lillian, have your true beginning? After that, we will move forward to your birth, your salvation, your death, and glory!

Let me put it another way. To really understand your future, we need to make a trip
into the past. I invite you, then, to go back in
time to your *true* beginning.

You see, if we began this inquiry at the point
of your death, we would actually be starting
in the *middle* of the story.

Take my hand, Lillian, and let's journey back a long, long way and find that moment of your beginning. How far back must we go? We will have to return to a point in time that predates the creation of Adam *and* even predates the creation of the world.

Did you exist *before* creation? Well, if you were just a body, the answer would be *no*. You would be only a temporal being, one who had a beginning and, of course, an end.

You also have a soul, and your soul will continue on after your body dies.

But you are not just a body and a soul (see 1 Thessalonians 5:23).

You are part spirit. This means part of you came from some place other than this *material* realm. The physical belongs to the physical world; the spirit belongs to the spiritual world. Your spirit had its beginning in the spiritual realm.

Are you mostly a body? Are you mostly a soul? Or is it possible that you are mostly a spiritual being? Without question, the most important part of you is your *spirit*.

It is difficult, is it not, to think of yourself as having a beginning that goes back to a time before you were born. Nonetheless, this is true of your *spirit*.

The physical part of you began years ago, when your *body* began. Your body is temporal, guaranteed *not* to last over one hundred years!

By the way, that may be the most exciting part of dying. Many years ago, you received a body that is now wearing out. That machine is destined to stop running. One day you will be rid of your temporal body forever!

What of your soul? Your soul began when your body did, but your soul, unlike your body, has no end. By definition, your soul is *everlasting*.

Everlasting means having a definite beginning but no end. Your soul began when you were conceived. You will give up your body, but you will continue on as an *everlasting* soul.

Things are definitely looking up. You will get rid of a worn-out body, and your soul will be set free.

But let's not stop there, because you are not *primarily* a body, neither are you *primarily* a soul. Nor was your true beginning on the day your mother gave birth to you, nor even when you were conceived. And your end is certainly not in a cemetery.

With that said, it is time to take a journey back to your true beginning. The best news of all awaits us there!

Shall our journey back through time take us as far back as the creation? Actually that is not far enough. We must now travel back to a place that is *before* even creation.

We are on our way to a place that existed before angels. We are going back to a time so remote it predates the existence of heaven. What could possibly have existed *before* creation? There is only one thing that existed *before* creation, and that is *God*.

Come. We have arrived at our destination. We have come to a place where God is everything! He is all there is. There is nothing else except God. Before creation, he is the *All*.

Now, Lillian, hold on tight, for we will dare to step *into* God!

Dare we? Yes. The Scripture assures us again and again that we are *in* him (e.g., Ephesians 2:19-22).

As we move into the very being of our God, we find ourselves in a realm where all things are light, where there is no such thing as death, where there is nothing temporal. There is nothing here that was created. Everything is uncreated. Everything is eternal. Everything is God! We are in life itself. Or should I say, "We are in Life himself!" His life goes on forever . . . in both directions. There never was when God was not. There never was when his life was not.

We stand in the realm of billowing revelation, light beyond all light. In him there is unhindered brightness. We stand engulfed in storms of incandescent glory.

What are we doing here, in a place before creation, where God is all? And dare we say that you, Lillian, had your beginning *here*?

Hold on even tighter! We are about to find the answer to that question, for we are about to plunge into the very center of the being of God.

Look around. Remember, we are now in a
time and place *before* creation. What you see
all around you is the very life of God. We are
surrounded by a life much higher than
human life could ever be.

It is in this mysterious place, and in this mysterious age, that God was making plans to
create. One of the things he decided to create
was you, Lillian. He had already thought up
the idea of giving you a body and a soul. But
he had also made another decision. Long
before your Lord ever began creating, he had
decided he would one day take a portion of

his very own life—a part of his life, which you see surrounding you now—and place that life . . . *his* life . . . in *you!*

Understand, it was way back here that God chose to put his *eternal* life inside you. He made that decision in that mysterious, distant age! He chose you before creation; he predestined that a portion of his being be placed *in* you.

And so, Lillian, *this* is where you began. In him. It was here, in him, that your Lord marked off a portion of his being to be placed *in* you.

Let me say that another way. It was way back here that God predestined you to become one of his children. The only way you (or I) can be the child of our parents is by having the life of our parents passed on to us. And the only way to be a child of God is to have his life passed on to us. And so it came about that your Lord marked off a portion of his very own being that would someday become *one* with you.

Do you know what that means? It means your spirit (the most important part of you) never had a beginning! There is a part of you that always has been, is, and always shall be. Part of you was . . . part of you is . . . part of you will be . . . eternal.

I will create the heavens. Then, on yet another day, I will create the earth. On still another day, a child, Lillian, will be born. This child of earthly parents is one whom I have chosen to be my own child. On a very special day, on the day of salvation, I will take this particular portion of myself and place it deep within her. This portion of my being will be the central essence of her person. From that moment of salvation she will carry within herself traits of my nature and my life.

Lillian will be unique among all my children and will express my divinity as no one else will. This portion of my life, which I have predestined to be in Lillian, will continue on . . . forever . . . from everlasting to everlasting.

Would you like to see that very portion of his divine nature which he purposed to place in you? Read on!

Do you see that pulsating, vibrating, glowing, shimmering element of God? Have you ever seen anything so beautiful, so flawless, so unutterably perfect? That is the portion of God which he has—here in eternity past—marked off *in* himself to be placed *in you*. You are looking at that portion of your Lord's divine nature which is destined to be placed in you and to become part of you in future time. When? To be exact, this portion of his being is destined to be planted in you at the time of your conversion. At that moment the very Spirit and life of God will become one with your spirit.

Look again and see that glorious portion of God, destined to be planted in you, to become one with you. Behold, the *real* you.

In the eyes of God, you are an eternal being. You have had a long, rich history . . . living in the center of the very vortex of God himself. A portion of you is in existence long before a little baby named Lillian is born. Later, at the time of your salvation, this very portion of the Lord's divine nature will come to live in you. And become one with you.

Reach out and touch that element of God, Lillian. Never forget just how beautiful, how indescribably beautiful, how holy, how pure this element of God is. Nor will that change when it enters into you at the time of your conversion. The beauty, purity, holiness, and perfection of that portion of God in you has not altered, and will not alter, throughout all your life as a Christian, nor will there be any change in his life on the day you die . . . or the day after, nor on into all the reaches of eternity. Never forget the purity, the perfection, and the glory you see here. And most of all, never forget that this portion of God— like all of God—can *never* die!

It is almost time for us to make our way back to space and time, to the physical creation, and to earth. Wouldn't it be nice if we Christians spent more time back here in eternity past, seeing how wonderful we are?

But just before we leave, there is something else here you should see.

You have now stood in that place, in God, where you existed *before* the foundation of the world. There is something else here that has to do with you. It is another event that took place before the foundation of the world.

Before we view this hallowed event, may I ask you some questions? Have you ever wondered why God chose you? What caused him to destine you to receive his eternal life? Why did he love you *that* much? Frankly, I do not know why he chose you, but I have always cherished that verse in the Old Testament that says of the people of Israel, "The Lord set his love upon you and chose you . . . because the Lord loves you" (Deuteronomy 7:7- 8, RSV). Perhaps the answer lies in that verse.

Have you ever doubted his love for you? Especially on a bad day when you were doing everything wrong? Our sinfulness can raise serious doubts in our minds about his love, can it not? Did you ever ask yourself, "What is God ever going to do with a believer as poor as I am?" Well, if you have done this, Lillian, you have wasted a lot of time worrying for nothing.

God chose you long before you were born. And long before you were born, he also took care of your sinful state. Can you grasp this? He took care of your sinful state before he created *anything*! Let me repeat that. He took care of the problem of your sin—and your sins—*before* creation.

Take my hand again. Let us visit that place where he took care of sin, and of death, too!

Do you see something up there ahead? Do you know what it is?

Come closer.

There!

That is "the Lamb that was slain from the creation of the world" (Revelation 13:8).

What can I say to you about this holy and sacred event, this incredible act of love . . . except to point out that a marvelous thing happened back here in the eternals that will later take care of all your needs.

Come, Lillian, for now it is time to journey *forward* in time. We are about to come to that place and to that very day when you were born from out of your mother's womb.

Do you recognize the young woman? That is your mother. She has just been handed a very beautiful baby. The baby, of course, is you.

Your body and soul, which had their beginning when you were conceived, have been thrust into the world. (Keep in mind that the body is guaranteed to last *no more* than a hundred years! The soul is guaranteed to go on forever.) Note the sparkling personality this newborn has. Yes, that is your soul shining its delightful personality out through your body. Your soul is already in tune with this realm of time and space. But keep looking, for there is more to see. Look deep inside that lovely little baby and you will see your spirit. Your very own personal, unique, human spirit.

But alas, Lillian, your spirit, which came from another realm, is not at home in this world. It has lost its vitality, for it is out of contact with the spiritual realm. It is like a limp balloon . . . even on the day you were born.

What is a newborn baby doing with something inside it that needs new life? Your human spirit needs new life because of the tragedy of the fall of Adam. Your ancestor, Adam, passed on to you (and to me, and to all the sons and daughters of Adam) a human spirit. But he also passed on to us the nature of sin.

When Adam was created, his spirit was very much alive. But his spirit died in the presence of sin. Since then, everyone who has ever come into this world has arrived with a *still-born* spirit. You and I, and all of us, make our entrance into this realm with something inside us that needs to be revitalized.

Well, we do not want to stop on that sad note, do we? There is a much better day out there that awaits you. Do you know what day I am talking about? The day you became a believer. That is the day your temporary body and your everlasting soul intersect with that wonderful *eternal* life that God marked off in himself before the foundation of the world.

Your God is, by nature, *spirit*. And after his Son, Jesus Christ, was raised from the dead, God came as a life-giving Spirit. This incredible life of God (*including* that part of him that was marked off for you and destined to become a part of you) . . . is life-giving. Right now that little baby has in it something that needs to have new life. That spirit needs to be made to live.

What will happen if that baby's spirit comes in contact with God's life-giving Spirit? Let's find out!

Do you recognize this place? What happened to you here?

Remember, we are making a journey through time. That is you, right over there. And this is the day of your conversion!

Look deep inside the young woman who is sitting there. See, the human spirit is still like a lifeless balloon—just as it was on the day she was born. But now turn around. Let us see what is happening *in* God!

A door in the heavenlies is opening. Do you recognize the scene? There is that portion of

God that was marked off before the creation of the world. Yes, that portion of God chosen to be placed inside *you*! That holy thing, so pure, so perfect . . . a portion of the very nature of God . . . is about to come inside you on this day of your redemption!

See! God's life is coming from out of that heavenly door and is passing through your body and soul. His life—his life-giving Spirit, his resurrecting life—is heading straight toward your spirit!

Remember, you had your real beginning *in God*. Well, right now that very portion of God is about to become one with you on this wonderful day.

What you are seeing is that mysterious event that is called "being born from above." Your spirit is inside your body and soul. God's life is about to touch your spirit. In mystery beyond mystery you are about to receive the Lord . . . inside you . . . forever.

The greatest single event of your life is about to take place. Part of God, marked off in himself so long ago, has now touched your lifeless spirit!

See! Incredible!

Resurrection!

Your human spirit has been brought to life, by *his* life! Part of you just rose from the dead! Isn't that wonderful! But that is not the end of wonder. There is more. Keep looking. Watch! His life, his Spirit, is now becoming *one* with your spirit.

Your spirit was made alive when God's life and Spirit touched your spirit. Now your *resurrected* spirit is coming into *oneness* with the life of God. From this moment, the two are inseparable. Your spirit and his Spirit have just become *one*. Forever!

We will leave this place now. But keep this in mind: There is a part of you that has been resurrected from the dead, and there is also a part of you that has come from the spiritual realm and from out of God himself. His eternal Spirit has never known death and will never know death, and that Spirit is one with *your* resurrected spirit.

Yes, a time will come, soon enough, when you will lay aside your body. But the most important part of you, your spirit—made one with God's life and God's Spirit—will *never* taste death.

What will happen in that moment when you breathe your last breath?

Actually, when Death comes he will have very little he can claim. He cannot claim your human spirit, for it has been resurrected from the dead. (And it is one with God!) *Nothing* dies *twice*. What else, then, can he claim? Death cannot claim God's life in you, simply because God's life cannot die. Death cannot claim your soul, for it has been redeemed . . . redeemed by the blood of the Lord Jesus.

What is there left for Death to claim? Not much! He can claim only that which you are probably very willing, at this point, to let him have. He *can* claim that temporary body of yours.

He gets precious little, does he not?

Have you ever realized just exactly what you are bequeathing to Death? He gets a worn-out body and, with it, sin, which dwells in the members of your body.

You leave to him nothing more than sin and all past remembrances of the Fall. *That* is what Death gets. You might say that you, not Death, get the last laugh.

And even as you render up to him your body, at that very moment you receive *the hope of glory!*

I think you know what takes place after that.

"We . . . would prefer to be away from the body and at home with the Lord" (2 Corinthians 5:8).

Your soul and your spirit (with the life of God in your spirit), at that moment, are set free.

Do you remember what we saw back there on the day you became a believer? God's life passed from the spiritual realm and came into you, there to become one with your spirit. At the moment of death, the scene reverses itself. You pass out of the physical realm, back through that door, and once again enter into the spiritual realm . . . into that realm where you really began! You will return "home" to the spiritual realm, to the place your spirit came from.

I have a notion the first face you will see as you pass through that door and enter the realm of the heavenlies will be that of a Man. You know him as your Lord and Savior.

You are going to meet a Man in the heavenlies. A physical, *visible* human being in a realm
where everything else is invisible and spiritual.

How is that possible?

Your Lord has already received his glorified
body—a body that can be seen with the
human eye—yet his body has all the properties
of the spiritual realm. His physical body has
become like his spirit. The body, the soul, and
the spirit of your Lord are so much one that
the physical and spiritual elements cannot be
separated. Look well upon your Lord . . . and
know in that moment that you will be like him!

Having laid aside a worn-out body, but with
a spirit that is alive and back home, you will
be able to look upon the very face of God, in
all his ultimate glory.

Exactly *where* does all this take place? Quite
frankly, I do not know the name of the place.

Jesus once said to the dying thief, "Today you will be with me in *paradise.*" Paul said he preferred, "to be away from the body and at home with the Lord." Will you be in a place called paradise, which, I assume, is some glorious part of the heavenly realm? Or are paradise and heaven one and the same? I do not know. I can only tell you this. You will be with him. Nothing else matters.

How long will you have to wait until the Lord returns to earth with the vast host of the redeemed and with the angels? Not long at all—not long for you, not long for Paul, not long for Abraham—for you will be living in a realm where there is no such thing as time.

And what will it be like when the Lord and you (and an innumerable host of angels and redeemed) return to this planet?

Let us see.

There will be at least one hundred million angels coming with you (Revelation 5:11; Matthew 25:31). Add to that all of the redeemed who have gone on before (1 Thessalonians 4:14). That should be quite a sight!

Imagine! You, standing in the heavenlies with that vast host, waiting for the door between our two realms to open!

Gabriel will blow his trumpet, and the Lord will give a shout that will split the foundations of creation. With that, he will descend (with the redeemed and the angels in his train) to claim his own who are still on earth.

As you near the earth, you will experience the *other* greatest moment you will ever live.

You are going to receive a body that is like his—wholly physical, yet completely spiritual. Think of it! You will have a body and a soul that have become like your spirit.

At last, dear Lillian, you will be complete.

In that moment, you will have received full salvation! You will be as flawless, perfect, pure, and whole in your body and soul as you are right now in your spirit. You will be a completed child of the living God.

As you approach this planet, you will see some incredible things happening down here on earth. The redeemed ones here on earth are going to see their decaying, sin-filled

bodies change in the twinkling of an eye.
Then they are all coming up to meet you!

And, oh, what a meeting that will be!

That will be the most spectacular moment
that has ever been or ever will be.

What then?

I would like to tell you that I understand
everything I am about to say, but I do not.

First of all, there will come forth a new earth
to replace this old one (Revelation 21).

Then comes the most exciting part . . . and
the most mysterious. All who are redeemed
are going to become one.

It appears, at least to me, that in our gathering
together and becoming one, we shall find that
we have become, all together, a *girl*—one glorious, beautiful, betrothed girl! (Ephesians 5:32).

Who is this beautiful, flawless young woman?

She is the most beautiful woman who has ever lived. She will carry within her all the gifts of her Lord. She will combine all of the personal traits of the God who gave her his life. All those portions of divine nature, which were placed in each one of the redeemed ones, will now join together and make one complete, glorious *counterpart* for the Lord.

Radiating out from the young woman, so pure and perfect, will flow forth the second greatest glory that will ever be known.

Who is this girl?

She is the bride of the Lord Jesus Christ. And *you* are a part of her! There you are . . . in her. A glorious girl . . . perfect, holy, pure, without spot or blemish.

What takes place next is beyond all understanding and all telling. This lovely girl, more beautiful than anything that all words or poetry could ever describe, will then become *one* with her Lord! (see Ephesians 5:22-33).

At that indescribable moment, you will return to that place where you began. Isn't that amazing! We are all going back to where we came from! The Lord Jesus and his bride will become utterly one. He who is the All will become the All in All. You will find yourself once more in the very center and vortex of God.

And you will be one with him forever more.

Hallelujah!

Love, *Gene*

P.S. *Lillian, if you really do precede me, when you arrive please give everyone my greetings. And tell Mother I'll soon be there.*

The Ship

I am standing upon the seashore and see a
nearby ship spread her white sails to the
morning breeze and start for the blue ocean.

She is an object of beauty and strength. I
watch her until at length she is only a speck
of white cloud just where the sea and sky
meet and mingle. Then someone at my side
exclaims, "She's gone!"

Gone where? Gone from my sight, that is all.
She is just as large in hull and mast and spar

as she was when she departed and just as able to bear her load of living freight to the place of her destination. Her diminished size is in me, not in her.

And just at the moment when someone cries "She's gone," there are other eyes watching for her arrival, and other voices that take up the glad shout, "There she comes!"

And that is dying.

—Author Unknown

References

Even though I walk
  through the valley of the shadow of death,
I will fear no evil,
  for you are with me;
your rod and your staff,
  they comfort me.

Surely goodness and love will follow me all the
      days of my life,
and I will dwell in the house of the Lord forever.
Psalm 23:4, 6

But God will redeem my life from the grave; he
  will surely take me to himself. *Selah*
Do not be overawed when a man grows rich,
  when the splendor of his house increases;

for he will take nothing with him when he dies,
his splendor will not descend with him.

Psalm 49:15-17

A good name is better than fine perfume,
and the day of death better than the day of birth.
It is better to go to a house of mourning
than to go to a house of feasting,
for death is the destiny of every man;
the living should take this to heart.

Ecclesiastes 7:1-2

On this mountain the Lord Almighty will prepare
a feast of rich food for all peoples,
a banquet of aged wine—
the best of meats and the finest of wines.

On this mountain he will destroy
the shroud that enfolds all peoples,
the sheet that covers all nations;
he will swallow up death forever.
The Sovereign Lord will wipe away the tears
from all faces;
he will remove the disgrace of his people
from all the earth.

The Lord has spoken.

In that day they will say,
    "Surely this is our God;
we trusted in him, and he saved us.
This is the Lord, we trusted in him;
    let us rejoice and be glad in his salvation."

Isaiah 25:6-9

Everyone who believes in him may have eternal life.

For God so loved the world that he gave his one
and only Son, that whoever believes in him shall
not perish but have eternal life.

John 3:15-16

I tell you the truth, whoever hears my word and
believes him who sent me has eternal life and will
not be condemned; he has crossed over from
death to life. I tell you the truth, a time is coming
and has now come when the dead will hear the
voice of the Son of God and those who hear will
live. For as the Father has life in himself, so he
has granted the Son to have life in himself. And
he has given him authority to judge because he is
the Son of Man.

Do not be amazed at this, for a time is coming when all who are in their graves will hear his voice and come out.

John 5:24-29

Do not store up for yourselves treasures on earth, where moth and rust destroy, and where thieves break in and steal. But store up for yourselves treasures in heaven, where moth and rust do not destroy, and where thieves do not break in and steal. For where your treasure is, there your heart will be also.

Matthew 6:19-21

Therefore I tell you, do not worry about your life, what you will eat or drink; or about your body, what you will wear. Is not life more important than food, and the body more important than clothes? Look at the birds of the air; they do not sow or reap or store away in barns, and yet your heavenly Father feeds them. Are you not much more valuable than they? Who of you by worrying can add a single hour to his life?

Matthew 6:25-27

My sheep listen to my voice; I know them, and they follow me. I give them eternal life, and they shall never perish; no one can snatch them out of my hand.

John 10:27-28

There will be more rejoicing in heaven over one sinner who repents than over ninety-nine righteous persons who do not need to repent.

Luke 15:7 (See also the entire 15th chapter.)

Jesus said to her, "I am the resurrection and the life. He who believes in me will live, even though he dies; and whoever lives and believes in me will never die. Do you believe this?"

John 11:25-26

Then the King will say to those on his right, "Come, you who are blessed by my Father; take your inheritance, the kingdom prepared for you since the creation of the world."

Matthew 25:34

In the future you will see the Son of Man sitting

at the right hand of the Mighty One and coming
on the clouds of heaven.

Matthew 26:64

At that time men will see the Son of Man coming
in clouds with great power and glory. And he will
send his angels and gather his elect from the four
winds, from the ends of the earth to the ends of
the heavens.

Mark 13:26-27

Do not let your hearts be troubled. Trust in God;
trust also in me. In my Father's house are many
rooms; if it were not so, I would have told you. I am
going there to prepare a place for you. And if I go and
prepare a place for you, I will come back and take you
to be with me that you also may be where I am.

John 14:1-3

I will remain in the world no longer, but they
are still in the world, and I am coming to you.
Holy Father, protect them by the power of
your name—the name you gave me—so that
they may be one as we are one.

John 17:11

Then he said, "Jesus, remember me when you come into your kingdom."

Jesus answered him, "I tell you the truth, today you will be with me in paradise."

Luke 23:42-43

After the Lord Jesus had spoken to them, he was taken up into heaven and he sat at the right hand of God.

Mark 16:19

For if, by the trespass of the one man, death reigned through that one man, how much more will those who receive God's abundant provision of grace and of the gift of righteousness reign in life through the one man, Jesus Christ.

Romans 5:17

For the wages of sin is death, but the gift of God is eternal life in Christ Jesus our Lord.

Romans 6:23

If only for this life we have hope in Christ, we are to be pitied more than all men.

But Christ has indeed been raised from the dead, the firstfruits of those who have fallen asleep. For since death came through a man, the resurrection of the dead comes also through a man. For as in Adam all die, so in Christ all will be made alive. But each in his own turn: Christ, the firstfruits; then, when he comes, those who belong to him. Then the end will come, when he hands over the kingdom to God the Father after he has destroyed all dominion, authority and power. For he must reign until he has put all his enemies under his feet. The last enemy to be destroyed is death. For he "has put everything under his feet." Now when it says that "everything" has been put under him, it is clear that this does not include God himself, who put everything under Christ. When he has done this, then the Son himself will be made subject to him who put everything under him, so that God may be all in all.

1 Corinthians 15:19-28

But someone may ask, "How are the dead raised? With what kind of body will they come?" How foolish! What you sow does not come to life unless it dies. When you sow, you do not plant the body that will be, but just a seed, perhaps of wheat or of something else. But God gives it a body as he has determined, and to each kind of seed he gives its own body. All flesh is not the same: Men have one kind of flesh, animals have another, birds another and fish another. There are also heavenly bodies and there are earthly bodies; but the splendor of the heavenly bodies is one kind, and the splendor of the earthly bodies is another. The sun has one kind of splendor, the moon another and the stars another; and star differs from star in splendor.

So will it be with the resurrection of the dead. The body that is sown is perishable, it is raised imperishable; it is sown in dishonor, it is raised in glory; it is sown a natural body, it is raised a spiritual body.

If there is a natural body, there is also a spiritual body. So it is written: "The first man Adam became a living being"; the last Adam, a life-giving spirit. The spiritual did not come first, but the natural, and after that the spiritual. The first man was of the dust of the earth, the second man from heaven. As was the earthly man, so are those who are of the earth; and as is the man from heaven, so also are those who are of heaven. And just as we have borne the likeness of the earthly man, so shall we bear the likeness of the man from heaven.

I declare to you, brothers, that flesh and blood cannot inherit the kingdom of God, nor does the perishable inherit the imperishable. Listen, I tell you a mystery: We will not all sleep, but we will all be changed—in a flash, in the twinkling of an eye, at the last trumpet. For the trumpet will sound, the dead will be raised imperishable, and we will be changed. For the perishable must clothe itself with the imperishable, and the mortal with immortality. When the perishable has been clothed with the imperishable, and the mortal with immortality, then the saying that is written will come true: "Death has been swallowed up in victory."

"Where, O death, is your victory? Where, O death, is your sting?"

1 Corinthians 15:35-55

Now we know that if the earthly tent we live in is destroyed, we have a building from God, an eternal house in heaven, not built by human hands. Meanwhile we groan, longing to be clothed with our heavenly dwelling, because when we are clothed, we will not be found naked. For while we are in this tent, we groan and are burdened, because we do not wish to be unclothed but to be clothed with our heavenly dwelling, so that what is mortal may be swallowed up by life. Now it is God who has made us for this very purpose and has given us the Spirit as a deposit, guaranteeing what is to come.

Therefore we are always confident and know that as long as we are at home in the body we are away from the Lord. We live by faith, not by sight. We are confident, I say, and would prefer to be away from the body and at home with the Lord.

2 Corinthians 5:1-8

Even as he selected us in him before the foundation of the world, having marked us out for adoption through Jesus Christ.

Ephesians 1:4-5 (See The New Testament:
An Expanded Translation [Wuest])

But whatever was to my profit I now consider loss for the sake of Christ. What is more, I consider everything a loss compared to the surpassing greatness of knowing Christ Jesus my Lord, for whose sake I have lost all things. I consider them rubbish, that I may gain Christ and be found in him, not having a righteousness of my own that comes from the law, but that which is through faith in Christ—the righteousness that comes from God and is by faith. I want to know Christ and the power of his resurrection and the fellowship of sharing in his sufferings, becoming like him in his death, and so, somehow, to attain to the resurrection from the dead.

Philippians 3:7-11

But our citizenship is in heaven. And we eagerly await a Savior from there, the Lord Jesus Christ, who, by the power that enables him to bring everything under his control, will transform our lowly bodies so that they will be like his glorious body.

Philippians 3:20-21

For you died, and your life is now hidden with
Christ in God. When Christ, who is your life,
appears, then you also will appear with him in glory.

Colossians 3:3-4

Brothers, we do not want you to be ignorant
about those who fall asleep, or to grieve like the
rest of men, who have no hope. We believe that
Jesus died and rose again and so we believe that
God will bring with Jesus those who have fallen
asleep in him. According to the Lord's own
word, we tell you that we who are still alive, who
are left till the coming of the Lord, will certainly
not precede those who have fallen asleep. For the
Lord himself will come down from heaven, with
a loud command, with the voice of the archangel
and with the trumpet call of God, and the dead
in Christ will rise first. After that, we who are
still alive and are left will be caught up together
with them in the clouds to meet the Lord in the
air. And so we will be with the Lord forever.
Therefore encourage each other with these
words.

I Thessalonians 4:13-18

The Lord will rescue me from every evil attack and will bring me safely to his heavenly kingdom. To him be glory for ever and ever. Amen.

2 Timothy 4:18

In bringing many sons to glory, it was fitting that God, for whom and through whom everything exists, should make the author of their salvation perfect through suffering. Both the one who makes men holy and those who are made holy are of the same family. So Jesus is not ashamed to call them brothers. He says,

I will declare your name to my brothers; in the presence of the congregation I will sing your praises.

And again,

I will put my trust in him.

And again he says,

Here am I, and the children God has given me.

Since the children have flesh and blood, he too shared in their humanity so that by his death he might destroy him who holds the power of death—that is, the devil—and free those who all their lives were held in slavery by their fear of death. For surely it is not angels he helps, but Abraham's descendants. For this reason he had to be made like his brothers in every way, in order that he might become a merciful and faithful high priest in service to God, and that he might make atonement for the sins of the people. Because he himself suffered when he was tempted, he is able to help those who are being tempted.

Hebrews 2:10-18

Now we who have believed enter that rest, just as God has said,

So I declared on oath in my anger,
   "They shall never enter my rest."

And yet his work has been finished since the creation of the world.

Hebrews 4:3

Their sins and lawless acts I will remember no more.

Hebrews 10:17

These were all commended for their faith, yet none of them received what had been promised. God had planned something better for us so that only together with us would they be made perfect.

Hebrews 11:39-40

But you have come to Mount Zion, to the heavenly Jerusalem, the city of the living God. You have come to thousands upon thousands of angels in joyful assembly, to the church of the firstborn, whose names are written in heaven. You have come to God, the judge of all men, to the spirits of righteous men made perfect.

Hebrews 12:22-23

He was chosen before the creation of the world, but was revealed in these last times for your sake.

1 Peter 1:20

But in keeping with his promise we are looking forward to a new heaven and a new earth, the home of righteousness.

2 Peter 3:13

And this is the testimony: God has given us eternal life, and this life is in his Son. He who has the Son has life; he who does not have the Son of God does not have life.

1 John 5:11-12

... written in the book of life belonging to the Lamb that was slain from the creation of the world.

Revelation 13:8b

Let us rejoice and be glad and give him glory! For the wedding of the Lamb has come, and his bride has made herself ready.

Revelation 19:7

Then I saw a new heaven and a new earth, for the first heaven and the first earth had passed away, and there was no longer any sea. I saw the Holy City, the new Jerusalem, coming down out of heaven from God, prepared as a bride beautifully dressed for her husband. And I heard a loud voice from the throne saying, "Now the dwelling of God is with men, and he will live with them. They will be his people, and God himself will be with them and be their God. He will wipe every tear from their eyes. There will be no more death or mourning or crying or pain, for the old order of things has passed away."

He who was seated on the throne said, "I am making everything new!" Then he said, "Write this down, for these words are trustworthy and true."

Revelation 21:1-5